SO..... THE MYSTERIES OF
ANCIENT ROME

Trudy Hanbury-Murphy

This paperback edition published in 2014
by Franklin Watts
338 Euston Road
London NW1 3BH

Franklin Watts Australia
Level 17/207 Kent Street
Sydney, NSW 2000

Copyright © 2014
Brown Bear Books Ltd

A CIP catalogue record for this book is available
from the British Library.

ISBN: 978 1 4451 3438 3

Dewey no. 937

Printed in China

Franklin Watts is a division of
Hachette Children's Books,
an Hachette UK company.
www.hachette.co.uk

Note to parents and teachers concerning
websites: In the book every effort has been
made by the Publishers to ensure that
websites are suitable for children, that they
are of the highest educational value, and that
they contain no inappropriate or offensive
material. However, because of the nature of
the Internet, it is impossible to guarantee that
the contents of these sites will not be altered.
We advise that Internet access is supervised
by a responsible adult.

Designer: Dave Allen
Picture Researcher: Clare Newman
Managing Editor: Tim Cooke
Indexer: Kay Ollerenshaw
Editorial Director: Lindsey Lowe

Contents

WHAT MADE ROME THE ETERNAL CITY?

THE CITY OF ROME ONCE RULED A MIGHTY EMPIRE. EVEN AFTER THE EMPIRE FELL, THE CITY REMAINED AT THE CENTRE OF EUROPEAN HISTORY.

History is everywhere in Rome. Ancient ruins rise above the streets. Holes in the ground mark sites where experts have discovered buried ruins.

Ancient pipes and drains beneath the city still provide running water to residents. It is no wonder that Rome is sometimes called the **Eternal** City. The name refers to its long history. A city has stood on the site for more than two thousand years.

A NEW DISCOVERY

Experts in **archaeology** have been studying Rome for the last two centuries. Discoveries are made all the time. In November 2007 archaeologists excavated the ruins of the palace of Augustus, who became Rome's first emperor in 27 BCE. Augustus built his palace on the Palatine Hill, at the heart of ancient Rome.

The Palatine was once crowded with buildings. Many collapsed over the centuries, and today the hill is full of hollows left by ancient ruins. To see if the ground beneath the palace was stable, the archaeologists drilled small holes in the ground near the walls.

Suddenly, the drill broke through into empty space. The archaeologists used a long probe to lower a camera into the hole. The camera revealed instantly that this was a very special discovery.

A Common Language

Latin was the language of the ancient Romans. They left written records of their life everywhere – not just plays and poems, but also histories and business records. Latin survives in **inscriptions** on ancient buildings. It is easy for experts to translate. Unlike many ancient languages, Latin has remained in use for thousands of years. Until the late twentieth century, it was taught in most schools.

The images from the probe showed a round chamber about 15 metres (50 feet) deep with walls covered in seashells, marble and **mosaics**. The decoration seemed too beautiful and expensive to belong to an ordinary home. The experts decided that the cave was probably a shrine for religious **rituals**.

SACRED CAVE

Accounts written by the Romans helped identify the site as the Lupercale, a place **sacred** to the ancient Romans. They

LEFT: *The Colosseum has become a symbol of Rome. When it was built in 80 CE, it could seat up to 50,000 people.*

Reconstructing the Past

Archaeologists often use computer models to **reconstruct** ancient buildings to help understand how they were built and used. A laboratory at the University of California, Los Angeles, USA, used computer technology to create a 3-D model of the Colosseum in Rome. The model reveals that the upper tiers of the building were very narrow and dark. People going to and from their seats must have moved around slowly.

Beneath the floor of the **arena** was a network of tunnels and cages. Animals and **gladiators** were held here. Lifts brought animals into the arena through trap doors. A system of pipes was used to flood the arena with water to stage naval battles.

BELOW: *Precise measurements from the ruins of the Colosseum enabled experts to create a 3-D reconstruction that showed how cramped parts of the building were for spectators.*

linked the cave to the founding of Rome. According to legend, the twins Romulus and Remus were the sons of the god Mars and the priestess Rhea. They floated down the River Tiber in a basket until a female wolf found them. The wolf nursed the twins in her cave on the Palatine Hill. In Latin, the language of ancient Rome, *lupa* means 'she wolf'.

A shepherd found the boys and raised them. On April 21, 753 BCE, when they were grown up, the twins founded a town at the site of the wolf's cave. They soon argued, however. Romulus killed Remus and became the

ABOVE: *This painting from about 1600 shows Romulus marking out the original boundaries of the city of Rome.*

first king of the town, which he called Rome, after himself.

The wolf's cave was seen as the birthplace of Rome. Some archaeologists believe that the cave beneath the palace is indeed the Lupercale and reason that Augustus intentionally built his palace on top of the sacred site. Others disagree. They argue that it is more likely to be a highly decorated tomb. Until more careful investigation work is done, the precise purpose of the chamber remains a mystery.

ABOVE: *The rich decoration on the walls of the Lupercale make some experts think it was a sacred place.*

A CITY OF ANCIENT RUINS

Not all new discoveries in Rome are as spectacular as the Lupercale. But they all add to experts' knowledge that, from 27 BCE until 476 CE, Rome was the centre of one of the largest **empires** the world has ever seen. So many ancient sites are buried beneath the streets of the modern city that ruins and **artefacts** constantly turn up during construction projects. Archaeologists have to assess all construction work to make sure that it will not damage ancient treasures.

Many of Rome's ancient buildings are close to the city centre. The city's most visible **monument** is the Colosseum. This huge arena was once used to stage fights between gladiators, among other entertainment. There are also many important ruins around the Roman **forum**. The forum was a space used for business, shopping, government and worship. It was home to temples, statues and government buildings.

EXPERT ENGINEERS

One of the best preserved of Rome's ancient monuments is the Pantheon. Although it has been standing for two thousand years, it still has its roof. The Pantheon was the only temple that honoured all of Rome's many gods. The Pantheon shows the skill of Roman builders. Its dome is made of a kind of concrete that is strong but also very light. At the top, the concrete is just 10 centimetres (4 inches) thick.

The emperors who ruled Rome from the first to fourth centuries CE wanted to ensure that the city was powerful and wealthy. Two million people lived in Rome, so even providing basic needs was difficult. A network of pipes and **aqueducts** carried water into Rome from springs far outside the city for drinking and bathing.

Many Roman emperors created great public buildings, such as bathhouses and temples. The city became a marvel of engineering. Augustus himself once claimed that he found Rome a city of brick but left it a city of marble.

BELOW: *The Roman forum was the ceremonial centre of ancient Rome. Today it is one of the most investigated archaeological sites in the world.*

WHO BUILT THE CITY?

THE ROMANS WERE JUST ONE GROUP OF PEOPLE IN CENTRAL ITALY BEFORE THEY BEGAN TO EXPAND THEIR INFLUENCE OVER THEIR NEIGHBOURS.

Rome sits on the banks of the River Tiber. In the tenth century BCE the site was home to farming peoples known as Latins and Sabines. The land was fertile and good for growing crops. It also attracted invaders. The Latins and Sabines clashed with their neighbours, the Etruscans, who took over the city. Etruscan culture was well developed.

They had their own king, language and religion. They used ships to trade throughout the eastern Mediterranean.

After a long series of clashes, the Latins and Sabines took back control of their land. They created a **republic**, governed by citizens rather than by a king. Two bodies took government decisions: a **senate**, with members of

RIGHT: *An archaeologist cleans mud from a pot found on a sunken Roman ship. Artefacts from shipwrecks are particularly useful for tracing trade routes.*

influential families of landowners, and an assembly made up of ordinary working people.

REPUBLICAN ROME

The Roman Republic soon became larger and more powerful. The Romans expanded both by defeating their neighbours in battle and by making alliances with them. They might offer to help a city by providing troops during a time of war, for example. When the war was over, the Romans left soldiers in the city to help protect it. Eventually, such military occupation brought the cities under Rome's control. In this way Rome gradually took over central and

LEFT: *This dome-shaped tomb was built by the Etruscans. The Romans learnt from the Etruscans, copying building techniques.*

southern Italy. The republic absorbed the newly conquered lands. Rome gave its new citizens the right to vote – but it also collected **taxes** from them. Rome grew very rich. Wherever legions of

Dating Remains

In 2006, **excavations** in the Roman forum uncovered a tomb with artefacts that dated from about 1000 BCE. That was far earlier than the legendary founding of the city. Other excavations revealed that in the late seventh century BCE, soon after the legend says the city was founded, the forum was paved with gravel. This suggests that peoples of the area had united and begun to build a more permanent settlement.

ABOVE: *One of seventeen Roman ships discovered at Pisa in 1998. They were so well preserved that experts could identify their cargoes, including wine, olive oil and fruit.*

BELOW: *These storage jars at the city of Ostia, southwest of Rome, stored grain from around the Mediterranean before it was taken up the River Tiber to Rome.*

Roman soldiers went, traders soon followed. New territory was knitted into a thriving network of trade centred on Rome. As the republic expanded outside Italy, Rome came to dominate the Mediterranean Sea. The Romans called the sea *Mare Nostrum* – 'Our Sea'.

EXPANDING ROME'S INFLUENCE

For three hundred years, Rome fought to increase its territory. It conquered what are now Greece, Turkey, France, Spain, Carthage in North Africa and Syria in West Asia.

The Romans organised their new lands as provinces. Each province was ruled by

a governor chosen by the senate. Soldiers from the legions were given land in the conquered territories as payment for their service. The soldiers settled in the provinces, where they introduced Roman customs. Many of the conquered people began to adopt these new ideas and to live as the Romans did. The Romans were not only conquering territory, they were also spreading their beliefs and ways of life.

FROM THE REPUBLIC TO THE EMPIRE

Rome's military success and wealth caused tension and jealousy among its leaders. Members of the senate began fighting among themselves. They came from powerful families that wanted to seize conquered lands for themselves. The senate split into competing groups, all eager for opportunities to increase their power and wealth. Eventually, the leaders of the army started to control Rome. The military leaders ruled as dictators. They ignored the senate and assembly when they wanted to. Julius Caesar was the most famous dictator. In 27 BCE, one of Caesar's descendants

Marine Archaeology

Experts who study underwater sites, such as flooded harbours or shipwrecks, are called marine archaeologists. These trained divers work in a similar way to archaeologists on land. They carefully record the location of everything they find with photographs or drawings. To get heavy objects to the surface, they attach balloons to them, which are then inflated. Some artefacts are waterlogged, so they need to be carefully treated to preserve them.

declared himself emperor, taking the title *Augustus*. The Roman Republic was over, and the Roman Empire was born.

RIGHT: *Archaeologists investigate the cargo of a Roman ship wrecked in the Mediterranean Sea.*

WHERE DID THE ROMANS LIVE?

AT ROME'S HEIGHT, MILLIONS OF PEOPLE IN EUROPE, WEST ASIA AND NORTH AFRICA COULD CLAIM "CIVIS ROMANUS SUM" – "I AM A CITIZEN OF ROME".

In 117 CE the Roman Empire reached its greatest extent. It stretched from Spain in the west to modern Syria and Israel in the east, and from Egypt in the south to the border of Scotland in the north. The Romans had spread their control along the whole coast of North Africa. They had conquered most of western and central Europe.

As new lands were absorbed into the Empire, their citizens often benefitted. The Romans built roads and ports to encourage trade, for example. Roman legions offered protection from bandits and pirates. Still, many people resented being ruled by their Roman conquerors. The Empire was now so large that it was difficult to control.

BELOW: *Hadrian's Wall followed natural features, such as cliffs, to create a barrier between the Roman Empire and the Picts to the north in modern-day Scotland.*

Roman Roads

Long, straight roads still exist all over the former Roman Empire. Most follow original Roman routes. The Roman road network extended 80,000 kilometres (50,000 miles). Roads were built as straight as possible and were used to send orders and messages, to transport goods and to move soldiers rapidly in case of an emergency. Most roads were built by Roman soldiers and funded by the army or by Rome itself.

HADRIAN'S BUILDINGS

When Hadrian became emperor in 117 CE the Roman Empire had forty-four provinces. Hadrian visited all but four of them. He was anxious to see that the Empire was being governed well.

Hadrian began many building projects. One of the most famous now bears his name – Hadrian's Wall, which lies along the old border of England and Scotland. The wall was 125 kilometres (73 miles) long and ran from coast to coast across a narrow part of Britain. It had small forts spaced every mile and larger forts at regular intervals. Hadrian built the wall to protect the northern border of the Empire. He wanted to prevent attacks by the Picts who lived to the north.

ABOVE: *The Roman baths in Bath, England, stood on the site of a spring that was a shrine for ancient Britons, who believed that the water had healing qualities.*

RUINS AND RECORDS

Archaeologists have found evidence throughout the Roman Empire of how different emperors tried to hold the Empire together. They often ordered the repair of old structures or built new ones to make life easier. Architects and engineers built bridges over rivers to improve transportation, aqueducts to provide water, harbours for ships and roads for wagons.

Towns and cities throughout the Empire began to resemble Rome itself. Buildings everywhere reflected the Roman style. They included theatres and colosseums, circuses for chariot races, marketplaces, bathhouses and temples.

One of the main purposes of public buildings was to encourage people to lead a Roman way of life. The emperors believed this would help keep even far-flung cities in the Empire loyal to Rome.

A TELL-TALE CLUE

Archaeologists excavating Roman buildings often have an invaluable clue to when they were built – buried coins. The same coins, called denarii, were used throughout the Empire. After 27 BCE, they were all marked with the head of the current emperor. When the coins turn up in excavations, they are a handy way of dating the layer of ground in which they are found.

Writing Home

In 1970 archaeologists discovered nearly 1,000 letters at a Roman fortress along Hadrian's Wall at Vindolanda in Britain. The letters were written on thin wood sheets with ink made from soot. They give us a glimpse of life for Roman soldiers based overseas. One letter is a birthday invitation. Others mention children, and some fragments seem to be children's writing exercises. More official letters grant leaves of absence or outline rules for the distribution of grain. Many letters were written to families back in Rome. Soldiers asked for warmer clothes, hunting nets, food or beer – anything that might make life more comfortable in chilly northern Britain.

LEFT: *The Vindolanda letters were written on thin sheets of wood. Paper, which the Romans made from reeds, was too expensive for everyday use.*

The Roman Army

The Roman Empire depended on the army. The army was a strong fighting force that was virtually unbeatable on open ground. Roman soldiers had to undergo strict training. They were expected to be fit enough to march as many as 32 kilometres (20 miles) per day. They had to have enough discipline to advance towards the enemy in close formations and to fight at close quarters. A particularly skilled soldier became a centurion and commanded a century – eighty infantrymen, or legionaries. A legion comprised fifty-nine centuries, and the army was made up of thirty

RIGHT: *An artist's reconstruction of a Roman centurion in uniform.*

?

DID YOU KNOW

On the battlefield, Roman soldiers locked their shields together above their heads to create a protective formation known as a 'tortoise'.

RIGHT: *This helmet was dropped by a Roman soldier fleeing from Germanic warriors at Teutoburg Forest.*

legions. There were also auxiliary troops who helped with various duties. They were often recruited from the conquered peoples of the Empire.

LEARNING ABOUT THE ARMY

Experts learn about how the Romans fought from clues buried on ancient battlefields. In Teutoburg Forest in Germany, an amateur archaeologist discovered the site of a famous Roman loss. Three legions were defeated by an army of German warriors. Fragments of metal armour, spearheads and broken weapons lay scattered where they had been dropped by Romans fleeing from the battle.

The Romans' weapons included a short sword for stabbing, a spear called a pilum and a large rectangular shield. Body armour was made with overlapping metal bands.

Roman writers provide another source of information about the Roman army. The defeat at Teutoburg was written about by Suetonius. He described how shocked Emperor Augustus was. The historian Ammianus Marcellinus had been a soldier himself. His account of a battle at Hadrianople in Turkey is important because he described exactly how the legions fought.

Famous Campaigns

The Roman army's most important campaigns included:

ca 215–148 BCE	Macedonian Wars, Greece
ca 274 -146 BCE	Punic Wars, Africa, Italy, Sicily
ca 192–188 BCE	Seleucid Wars, Asia Minor
ca 58–50 BCE	Gallic Wars, France
55 BCE	Invasion of Britain
114–166 BCE	Parthian Wars, Mesopotamia

HOW DID THE ROMANS LIVE?

LIFE WAS HARD FOR POOR ROMANS, BOTH IN THE CITIES AND IN THE COUNTRYSIDE, BUT OTHER ROMANS ENJOYED A COMFORTABLE LIFESTYLE.

C lues about how the Romans lived come from a number of sources. One of the most important is physical ruins. In the centre of Rome itself, for example, stood the forum. This was originally a marketplace and a space where people met to celebrate Rome's military triumphs. The forum grew into the business centre of the city. Today it is a treasure trove for archaeologists.

BELOW: *A Roman amphitheatre at Pula in Croatia. Wherever the Romans settled, they built structures similar to those in Rome.*

They have found inscriptions that identify workshops and shops that belonged to florists, perfumers and jewellers. Parts of the forum were also sacred. Temples there were dedicated to deities such as Jupiter, god of the sky.

WRITERS' WORDS

Inscriptions, like those on monuments and coins, are useful tools for archaeologists. But there are many other sources of information about the Romans, too. They include ancient poets and playwrights who give us a glimpse of real life. In the second century BCE, the playwright Plautus described life in the forum. He mentioned moneylenders and gossips, as well as wealthy merchants. His accounts make it easy to imagine the hustle and bustle of the time.

The forum was not Rome's only public space. The Colosseum and the Circus Maximus were also popular. Battles with gladiators and animals were staged at the Colosseum. It could even be flooded to stage sea battles. The Circus Maximus held daily chariot races. The poet Juvenal complained that his fellow Romans were only interested in "bread and circuses" – eating and entertainment.

ABOVE: *This wall painting shows two kitchen slaves gutting a hare. Only wealthy Romans could afford to eat meat, including wild game, regularly.*

Food and Drink

The fertile lands of North Africa and those around the Mediterranean Sea supplied Rome with grain, olives and fruit. Staple foods such as bread, soup and beer were made from wheat or barley. Olive oil and wine from grapes were used by Romans and traded around the Empire. Overland trade routes brought spices such as cinnamon and pepper from Asia and Africa. These new spices were gradually added to Roman recipes.

Who to Trust?

Written sources can be helpful to archaeologists – but they only tell one side of the story. Accounts can vary depending on who wrote them. Julius Caesar wrote positive accounts of his military campaigns because he wanted to support his own political career. Meanwhile, Juvenal set out to criticise the emperors in a clever and funny way, so he pointed out their flaws. How people saw Rome depended on who they were.

ABOVE: *This Roman mosaic illustrating a Greek myth decorates a villa in what is now Tunis in Tunisia.*

HOME FROM HOME

Wherever they settled, the Romans took their home comforts. Most Roman towns had amphitheatres and circuses. The Romans also built bathhouses, often using natural springs. The baths were important as meeting places as well as places for washing. The Romans used steam rather than baths to get clean. Bathers moved through a series of rooms. The first was used for changing and scraping off dirt. The second room was very hot, so people would sweat and get rid of more dirt from the skin. The third room had a pool in which to cool down.

The hot room, or 'caldarium', was heated by a furnace. Hot air circulated through hollow walls and in a space beneath the floor called a **hypocaust**. A similar system was used to heat large **villas** in colder parts of the Empire.

Villas were the homes of wealthy families that were often located in the country outside the crowded cities and towns. Villas were arranged around a central courtyard. Their many rooms were decorated with frescoes, mosaics and statues. The writer Petronius described how wealthy Romans gathered in a villa for a feast. The diners lay on

BELOW: Olive trees on a hillside in Italy. Olives were one of the most valuable harvests in the Empire, both for the fruit and the oil they produced.

LEFT: The ruins of this Roman villa show the pillars of the hypocaust, which allowed hot air to circulate beneath the floor.

couches and were served by slaves. The banquet included olives, honey and baked **dormice** washed down with wine. Experts know about many other Roman recipes. A writer named Apicius wrote a cookbook that survives today.

Today, we have a clear picture of how the Romans lived. Experts can look at ruins, read ancient books and restore mosaics, frescoes and paintings. There is always more to be discovered. Any new discovery might make us reconsider what we know.

The Myth of Rome

Ancient Rome has had a hold over Western culture for centuries. Rome has influenced the way modern cities are built and governed. It has shaped major elements of the art, literature and philosophy of the West. Ancient Roman literature – which is often grouped with Greek literature and referred to as **classics** – is still widely studied in schools and universities.

Ancient Rome first became popular during the Renaissance, which lasted from the thirteenth to sixteenth centuries. Throughout Europe, particularly in Italy, scholars and artists revived learning based on the great achievements of the ancient

BELOW: *Eighteenth-century tourists visit an ancient Roman temple in France. Artists often tried to imitate what they saw as classical style.*

Greeks and Romans. Arts and education thrived during this period.

Starting in the seventeenth century, Rome became an important destination on the so-called Grand Tour. The tour was an extended trip taken by European or American students, usually wealthy young men, intended to educate the student about European culture. It usually included visits to Paris, Venice, Florence and Rome to study art and architecture.

Many visitors took home souvenirs of their travels. They included antiquities such as ceramics and statues. The relics of ancient Rome gradually spread across Europe, into stately homes and museums.

In the eighteenth century, revolutionaries in France were drawn to what they saw as the ideals of the Roman Republic – liberty and freedom. They used the republic as a model for their legal systems and government. They set out to make Paris a 'new Rome', building monuments with columns and triumphal arches. Supporters of the revolution were influenced by ancient Roman writers such as Cicero, Livy and Plutarch.

ABOVE: *Russell Crowe (left) fights in the film* Gladiator. *The film's popularity is proof of our continuing fascination with ancient Rome.*

Admiration for Roman values is still strong. *Gladiator*, a film set in ancient Rome, won five Oscars. It explores ideas about honour, revenge and bravery. Such values still strike a chord today.

WHY DID ROME FALL?

ROME'S SUCCESS MADE THE EMPIRE DIFFICULT TO HOLD TOGETHER. AFTER ONLY A FEW HUNDRED YEARS, ROME BEGAN TO LOSE ITS INFLUENCE.

The collapse of the Roman Empire is fascinating for historians. From its greatest extent in 117 CE, the Empire lasted only three hundred and fifty years. In 476 CE Romulus Augustus, the last western emperor, was forced from his post. By then, large areas of Rome lay empty and overgrown with weeds. The city's population had fallen to only 20,000. What had gone wrong?

There are many ideas. One suggests that many Romans were poisoned by lead used to make water pipes and wine barrels. That is unlikely, but some experts do believe that Romans may have suffered from new diseases from the farthest parts of the Empire.

BELOW: *An audience watches a play in a Roman theatre. Even people in the back row can hear the actors on stage.*

DECLINE OF THE EMPIRE

Most experts believe that the collapse of the Empire did not have one cause but many. One of the most important was that the Empire had simply become too big. It was difficult to govern effectively. The borders were so long that they were difficult to defend. The Romans called all peoples who were not included in the Empire **barbarians**. Far from Rome, barbarians began making more frequent raids on the Roman provinces.

Meanwhile, the position of the emperors in Rome had grown weaker as the senate and the army competed for power. In 186 CE soldiers strangled the emperor and appointed their own candidate. The army began selling the title of emperor to the highest bidder. Between 186 and 196 CE there were thirty-seven different emperors. Twenty-five of them were assassinated.

Without a strong ruler, the Empire would soon fall apart. In 395 CE Emperor Diocletian decided to split the Empire into western and eastern sections, each with its own emperor. He believed this would make governing the Empire easier. Rome would remain the capital of the Empire in the west. Constantinople (now Istanbul in modern-day Turkey) became capital of the Empire in the east. Diocletian appointed an army officer, Maximillian, to rule the Western Empire.

MORE PROBLEMS FOR ROME

It soon became apparent that the division of the Empire had not worked. The Empire in the west continued to grow weaker. It cost so much for the army to defend the Empire that there was little money left to repair and maintain key structures. Roads, bridges and public buildings began to fall into disrepair.

As barbarian raids into the Empire increased, the quality of the Roman army fell. It had fewer men. Many of its new recruits were untrained soldiers from throughout the Roman Empire. When the army fought, it was defeated in battles it may once have won.

The Past Under Threat

Roman ruins are under threat throughout Europe. One problem is that there are simply too many ruins. There are Roman sites in most major European cities. There are so many ruins that city planners and politicians argue that they cannot all be preserved. Modern life must go on, which means that houses and car parks must be built. All archaeologists can hope to do is to preserve the most important sites and to record the contents of other sites as much as possible before they are destroyed.

RIGHT: *Castel Sant'Angelo in Rome is often called Hadrian's tomb. The ancient tomb is actually buried beneath the castle.*

The Empire's economy was also weak. Rome was spending more than it could afford. As Rome lost control of various provinces, it could no longer collect taxes from them. The money flowing into the treasury decreased. There was such a shortage of gold that the emperors reduced the amount of gold used to make Roman coins. This led to a general increase in prices, known as **inflation**. Meanwhile, the emperors continued to spend money on luxuries such as silk and spices rather than trying to increase trade to maintain Rome's income.

THE END OF THE EMPIRE

Barbarians severely damaged the Roman economy with their raids on the Empire. Finally, in 476, German warriors called Visigoths entered and looted the city of Rome. The Visigoth king Theodoric deposed the Roman emperor Romulus Augustus and took over the rule of Italy. The Empire in the west was over.

BELOW: *Carved stone blocks at a Roman site in Turkey wait to be shipped to a museum to avoid being flooded after a dam was built on the River Euphrates in 2000.*

Throughout Europe, trade declined and people left the cities. The ability to speak Latin or to read at all became rare.

The Empire in the east was known as Byzantium. It survived until 1453, when it was defeated by the Ottoman Turks. Some historians date this as the end of the Empire. Most, however, do not see Byzantium as the true heir of the Roman Empire. In their eyes, Rome was already a thing of the past – although its glories would one day spread wonder again.

Further Resources

BOOKS

Bingham, Jane. *Explore! Romans.* Wayland, 2014

Hewitt, Sally. *Project History: The Romans.* Franklin Watts, 2013

Macdonald, Fiona. *History Crafts: Ancient Rome.* Franklin Watts, 2013

Malam, John. *History From Objects: The Romans.* Wayland, 2012

Nilsen, Anna. *Puzzle Heroes: Ancient Rome.* Franklin Watts, 2014

Townsend, John. *EDGE: Mad, Bad and Just Plain Dangerous: Romans.* Franklin Watts, 2013

WEB SITES

Visit the BBC history site about the ancient Romans.
http://www.bbc.co.uk/history/ancient/romans/

The BBC history site aimed at schoolchildren.
http://www.bbc.co.uk/schools/romans/index.shtml

The British Museum's website on ancient Rome, with links to detailed information about chariot racing.
http://www.britishmuseum.org/explore/world_cultures/europe/ancient_rome.aspx

A short video lesson about Roman life from Ted.com.
http://ed.ted.com/lessons/a-glimpse-of-teenage-life-in-ancient-rome-ray-laurence

The PBS site about ancient Rome
http://www.pbs.org/empires/romans/index.html

Glossary

aqueduct: A raised structure built to carry water.

archaeology: The scientific study of cultures by analysing remains such as artefacts and monuments.

arena: An area with seating for public entertainment.

artefact: An object that has been made or changed by humans.

barbarians: The name given to people who were not citizens of the Roman Empire.

classics: The literature of ancient Greece and Rome.

dormice: Small, mouse-like rodents.

empire: A large area of land in which different peoples are ruled by an emperor or empress.

eternal: Everlasting.

excavation: A scientific dig to explore an archaeological site.

forum: An open marketplace in a Roman city that was the centre of public life.

gladiator: A fighter trained to take part in public fights.

hypocaust: An ancient Roman heating system with an underground furnace.

inflation: A rise in prices over a period of time.

inscription: A word or phrase carved into a hard surface, such as stone.

monument: A structure built to celebrate a person, god or event.

mosaic: An image made from small pieces of coloured stone or glass.

reconstruct: To rebuild something as it looked in the past, using research and scientific data.

republic: A nation governed by officials who are elected by citizens.

ritual: A ceremony carried out as part of religious worship.

sacred: Something worthy of worship.

senate: The council that made laws in ancient Rome.

tax: A contribution paid by a citizen to the government for the services it provides.

villa: A large home in the country built by a wealthy Roman, often as a farm or a holiday home.

Index

Page numbers in **bold** type refer to captions.